#GirlHacks

#GirlHacks

Topanga Skye
Catia Mehring
Peaceful Daily Publishing

Copyright © 2015 by
Topanga Skye and Catia Mehring

All rights reserved.

No part of this book may be reproduced, copied, stored or transmitted in any form or by any means – graphic, electronic or mechanical, including photocopying, without the prior written permission of Peaceful Daily, except where permitted by law.

Library of Congress Control Number: 2015953479

Published by Peaceful Daily Publishing
www.peacefuldaily.com

ISBN 978-0-9884926-9-1

Book design by Perseus-Design.com

Special thanks to our favorite FROYO joint, Sweet Frog Premium Frozen Yogurt of Guilford, Connecticut, for supplying a great location for our cover photo shoot.

Printed in the United States of America.

First Edition

10 9 8 7 6 5 4 3 2 1

Dedicated to

Friends everywhere

(cuz u r never 2 old or young 4 a sleepover!)

Contents

Introduction	ix
Sleepovers	1
Happy Thoughts	5
Tech Tips	11
Beauty	23
Room Decor	39
Roaming	51
Fashion	55
School	67
About the Authors	79

Introduction

Welcome to our book, #gIrLHacKS. We are a couple of girls who were inspired to write a book of things we love and tips to help other girls our age. So here you have it...our first book! We are so proud of it, especially because we are donating $1 from the sale of every book to international charity *Free The Children*. They are committed to delivering a sustainable development model that empowers people to transform themselves, their families, their communities and the world.

Sleepovers

Sleepovers rock! Pulling an all-nighter is a blast but apply cucumbers to your eyes in the morning. No sleep can make eyes puffy!

#GIRLHACKS

Cool stuff to bring on your sleepover:

Pjs
Toothbrush/toothpaste
Phone (if you are lucky enough to have one)
Laptop
Makeup
Speakers
Movies
Pillows

Sleepovers

Stuff to do on your sleepover:

Watch movie
Truth or dare (of course everybody does dare at a sleepover)
Makeovers
Nails: see the Beauty section in our book
Campfire + s'mores (weather permitting)
Talk drama and school
Play on devices
Listen to music
Make a dance routine
DIYs
Look at magazines

#GIRLHACKS

Fun things to eat at sleepovers:

DIY ice cream
Brownies
Pizza
Baked cookies (make sure an adult is there too, OK?)
Chips
Gum
Pancakes
Smoothies
Waffles
French toast
Donuts

Happy Thoughts

Sometimes things can be a bummer. We have some life hacks for that, too!

#GIRLHACKS

Animals always find a way to make us happy! Having a bad day? Spend a few moments with a pet and watch how happy you become.

Happy Thoughts

Doing what you love is important. Figure out what you love and go do it! We love dancing and music. You probably do, too!

Nothing can make a rainy day better than putting on some headphones and listening to really loud music!

Happy Thoughts

Thinking good thoughts is important. When you are stressed always return to a favorite thought, like a happy memory or the face of a favorite person.

Tech Tips

We are so lucky to have technology! Imagine being a kid in the ancient times like our parents!

#GirlHacks

When taking a selfie, show your natural face with no makeup. Makeup on phone cameras looks worse than no makeup.

Tech Tips

Always use a password that is something that only you would know: an important date or number combo. Then write down a clue on a piece of paper like: "My phone passcode is the day we got my dog," or something. This way only you will know the answer.

#GIRLHACKS

Try to change your password as little as possible so it's less likely you'll forget it.

Tech Tips

If you have a phone or device, try to choose a case with a thick bumper (the case part around the screen). It will prevent the screen from cracking, but will always be more Tumblr with a skinny case!

#GIRLHACKS

If you have a pet at home that likes to chew on your phone charger, cover it with multiple layers of duct tape. It will make it look super cute and your pet won't bite through the duct tape!

Tech Tips

Buy a screen protector even if your screen isn't cracked. This way if you drop it, you won't have a cracked screen.

#GirlHacks

If you want a cute background, get an editing app or a background app.

Tech Tips

Get some cheap, plain phone cases and decorate them with permanent marker. Voila! You have a cute, customized phone case.

You can cover some of your keys on a laptop in washi tape. It gives a fun pop of color.

Tech Tips

Duck faces in a selfie are so out. It makes you look uncool.

Beauty

We are all individuals with natural beauty but being a tween has introduced us to a cool new world: makeup!

However, a smile is the best thing you can ever put on your face!

Blueberry Mask for Oily Skin

Put in blender and blend:

1 cup oatmeal
1 cup blueberries
1 tablespoon honey
10 almonds, whole

Spread on face and let dry! Rinse with warm water, and splash your skin with cool water afterwards!

Beauty

Don't apply blush to the lower half of your cheeks. It looks unnatural.

#GIRLHACKS

Cleanse your face every other day to prevent acne. Don't overdo it, though.

Apply darkest eye shadow shades to the lower half of your eyelids.

#GIRLHacKS

After applying lipstick, blot. Then reapply to make it last longer.

Beauty

Laughter is a big beauty YES. Good for us, we are always laughing.

#GIRLHACKS

Apply a clear coat of polish every two days for a lasting manicure.

Beauty

When applying a clear coat of polish to nails, focus on outer edges to avoid chipping.

Pastels and neons are in the now for nail color.

Beauty

Don't put on too much powder. It looks chalky.

Use honey on acne overnight. It will help it disappear.

Beauty

Don't rub your face because it causes acne. Hands off face!

#GIRLHACKS

Eating fresh fruits and veggies is good for your skin.

Beauty

Don't apply blush to your nose. It looks like you have a cold.

Room Decor

Our rooms rock! We love hanging in our rooms, listening to music, watching YouTube and group texting our friends!

#GIRLHACKS

Need help organizing your notes? Buy some cheap corkboards, whiteboards, and chalkboards to hang above your desk in a cute display.

Room Decor

Before you buy something for your room, make sure it goes with the color combo.

#GiRLHacKS

If you need some cheap, cute room decor, go to the thrift store and gussy up something there with spray paint, fabric, duct tape, etc.

Room Decor

If you have a messy desk drawer, get some shallow dishes to place in an array in the desk drawer to organize stuff.

#GIRLHACKS

If you happen to be a slob, schedule a day to clean your room every two weeks. After a while, you might find it fun. We certainly do.

Room Decor

If you're kind of sick of your room, try rearranging the furniture. It will make it look completely different.

#GirLHacKS

Fake flowers are a big YES. They are very cheap, add tons of color, and require no maintenance.

Room Decor

You can't have too many pillows!! They will brighten up your room and are sooo comfy!!

#GIRLHACKS

Perhaps you don't like the look of curtains for your open closet. You can look online for beaded strands. They look very boho and chic.

Room Decor

Faux fur is a YES. Especially white fur. It looks so cute and feels so comfortable.

Roaming

Going to new places is so inspiring!

#GIRLHACKS

Essentials for Roaming:

Hair brush + products
Makeup
Moisturizer
Camera/phone
Carry-on bag
Change of shoes
Toothbrush and toothpaste
Money (always have your own money)

Roaming

Places to go:

Beach
Big cities
Pool
Bowling Alley
Arcade

Fashion

You can never go wrong with a pair of ripped up jeans...

#GIRLHACKS

If you have a pair of jeans that are too short on you, roll the ankles up once or twice to make capris. You can even sew the sides of the fold.

Fashion

It's okay to wear two patterns at once (if they look good together), but make sure there is at least one common color in both patterns.

#GIrLHacKS

A run in your tights? Apply some clear nail polish around the end of the run to prevent it from spreading.

Fashion

Rub a nail file on your denim jeans or shorts to make them look more distressed.

#GiRLHacKS

If you have dark neutral colors on, add a fun pop of color with an accessory.

Fashion

Looking to spice up your wardrobe? Get some brightly colored eternity scarfs. They are really cute and you can really rock them with jeans and a sweater.

#GIRLHACKS

When shopping for clothes, make sure you know what you're looking for, and try to find clothes that go well with some of your other clothes.

Fashion

If you can't try on a pair of jeans in a store, place the pair around your neck; if you can meet both ends at the back of your neck, they will fit.

#GIRLHACKS

Spray your tights with hairspray to prevent holes and runs.

Fashion

Use hairspray to remove a lipstick stain.

School

It has its advantages.

Homework is not one of them.

#GirlHacks

When taking notes, color code. It makes it way easier to find the info you need.

School

Cover a paper folder in duct tape if it is ripped.

If you want a cheap and chic pocket for your locker, use duct tape again.

School

To keep your locker organized, keep a folder labeled "junk" in your locker. Whenever you have a paper that you DO NOT NEED, just dump it in there. Then at the end of the year you can just throw the whole thing in the trash.

#GIRLHACKS

Make sure to clean out your binders every week or two. You might have notices, permission slips, or tests that you need.

School

Want to hide money at school? Take an empty lip balm container, or just roll all the lip balm out. Then roll up your money and slip it in!

#GirlHacks

Keep an emergency pouch in your locker with lip balm, hair ties, band aids, roll-on perfume, and any other necessities.

School

Before you start school, make a couple of copies of your schedule. You can put one in your locker, tape one on your binder, etc. This way you'll never not know where to go.

#GIRLHACKS

Write down all of your assignments and test dates. This way you will know what to do when you get home.

School

When you have a deep secret, the only person you could get away with telling is your best friend(s). Sometimes even close friends can give it away.

About the Authors

Topanga Skye Corso

Hi, I am Topanga Skye, and my friends call me Top. I love watching videos on DIYs, makeup and decor tips. What I love even more is listening to my favorite songs and the top 10 songs of the week. I love music, art, dance, Instagram (@topangaskye) and doing makeup. I also LOVE animals and spending time with my cat named Wheatie and dog named Bosco! I loved writing this book! I can't wait to write more!

Catia Mehring

Hello! I am Catia Mehring and when this book was made, I was a Tween. When I grow up, I want to become a dancer. My best friends are Topanga (the other writer of this book) and my other friend, Izzy. I was looking for books similar to ours, but couldn't find any. I hope you enjoy this book just as much as Topanga and I enjoyed writing it!

About the Authors

Keep up with us...

Topanga/Catia
c/o Peaceful Daily Publishing
800 Village Walk
Suite 103
Guilford, CT 06437

Topanga Skye
www.topangaskye.com
Instagram @topangaskye
Youtube @topangaskye

Learn more about our favorite charity *Free The Children* at WE.org.

Your Happy Thoughts

www.ingramcontent.com/pod-product-compliance
Lightning Source LLC
Chambersburg PA
CBHW030604020526
44112CB00048B/1211